APR 4 2001

GLENDALE CALIF. PUBLIC LIBRARY 91205 CHILDREN'S ROOM

D0475218

GLENDALE PUBLIC LIBRARY
222 EAST HARVARD ST.
GLENDALE, CALIF. 91205

Tasting
in Living Things

Karen Hartley, Chris Macro, and Philip Taylor

Heinemann Library
Chicago, Illinois

j
c 612.87
HAR

©2000 Reed Educational & Professional Publishing
Published by Heinemann Library,
an imprint of Reed Educational & Professional Publishing,
100 N. LaSalle, Suite 1010
Chicago, IL 60602
Customer Service 888-454-2279

All rights reserved. No part of this publication may be reproduced or transmitted in any form or by any means, electronic or mechanical, including photocopying, recording, taping, or any information storage and retrieval system, without permission in writing from the publisher.

Designed by Celia Floyd
Illustrated by Alan Fraser
Originated by Ambassador Litho
Printed in Hong Kong / China

04 03 02 01 00
10 9 8 7 6 5 4 3 2 1

Library of Congress Cataloging-in-Publication Data
Hartley, Karen, 1949-
   Tasting in living things / Karen Hartley, Chris Macro, and Philip Taylor.
       p. cm. – (Senses)
   Includes bibliographical references and index.
   Summary: Describes how the sense of taste works in humans and animals and how they use it.
   ISBN 1-57572-250-X (lib. bdg.)
   1. Taste Juvenile literature. [1. Taste. 2. Senses and sensation.] I. Macro, Chris, 1940- . II. Taylor, Philip, 1949-
. III. Title. IV. Series: Hartley, Karen, 1949- Senses.
QP456.H27 2000
573.8'78—dc21   99-38257
                                                     CIP

Acknowledgments

The Publishers would like to thank the following for permission to reproduce photographs:

Bruce Coleman/Jane Burton, p. 22; Bruce Coleman/mpl Fogden, p. 17; Corbis/Kennard Ward, p. 16; FLPA/Winifred Wisniewski, p. 23; Heinemann/Gareth Boden, pp. 4, 5, 6, 7, 8, 11, 13, 15, 24, 25, 26, 27, 28, 29; Trevor Clifford, p. 10; Image Bank/P. Goetgheluck, p. 20; Oxford Scientific Films/Steve Turner, p. 18; Tom Ulrich, p. 21; Pictor International, p. 19; Tony Stone/Peter Cade, p. 19; Roy Gumpel, p. 9.

Cover photograph reproduced with permission of Oxford Scientific Films and Gareth Boden.

Every effort has been made to contact copyright holders of any material reproduced in this book. Any omissions will be rectified in subsequent printings if notice is given to the Publisher.

Some words are shown in bold, **like this**. You can find out what they mean by looking in the glossary.

CONTENTS

WHAT ARE YOUR SENSES?

Senses tell people and animals about the world around them. You use your senses to feel, see, hear, taste, and smell. Your senses make you feel good and warn you of danger.

Senses are important to you and other animals. This book is about the sense of taste. You will find out how taste works and what you use it for.

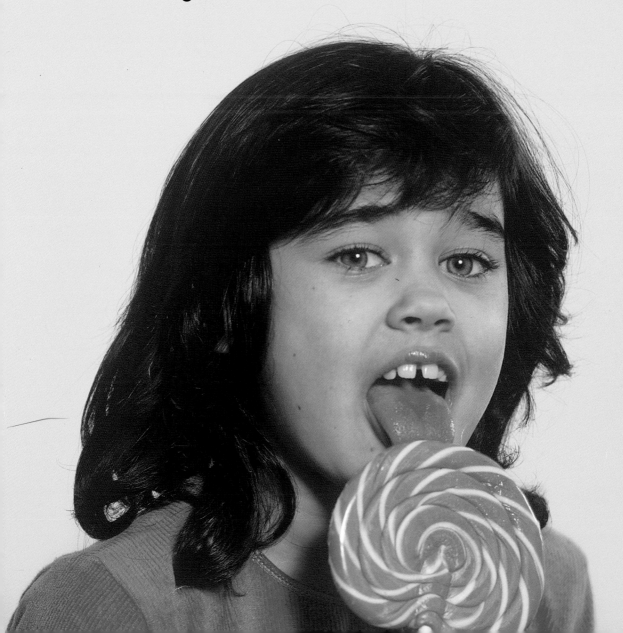

WHAT DO YOU USE TO TASTE?

Taste and smell work together to make **flavor**. Your **taste buds** sense **chemicals** in food. Your nose senses the smell. Together they send a message to the brain.

You taste things with your tongue. The tongue can only taste things when it is wet. **Saliva** keeps your mouth wet. The **roof** of your mouth can taste things, too.

HOW DO YOU TASTE THINGS?

You can only taste something if it is in your mouth or on your tongue. There are tiny lumps on the edges of your tongue and in your mouth called **taste buds**.

The picture shows the taste buds on a tongue. When they sense something, they send a message to the brain. Your brain remembers lots of different tastes.

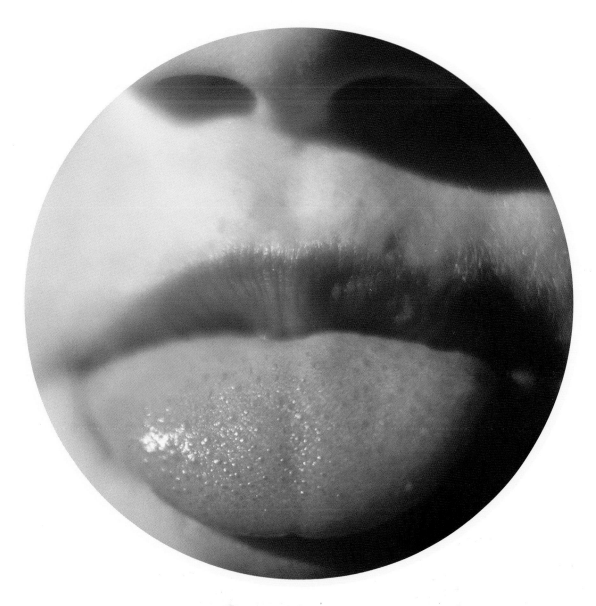

HOW DOES TASTE HELP YOU?

Taste tells your brain that something is in your mouth. You can only taste food when you can smell it. You eat food because you like the taste.

When you taste something that is not safe to eat, your brain tells you to spit it out. Your brain does not always recognize bad things. That is why you must not eat or drink things if you do not know what they are.

HOW DO YOU USE TASTE?

There are groups of **taste buds** on different parts of the tongue. There are different taste buds to taste salty things like potato chips, sweet things like sugar, sour things like lemon, and bitter things like green olives.

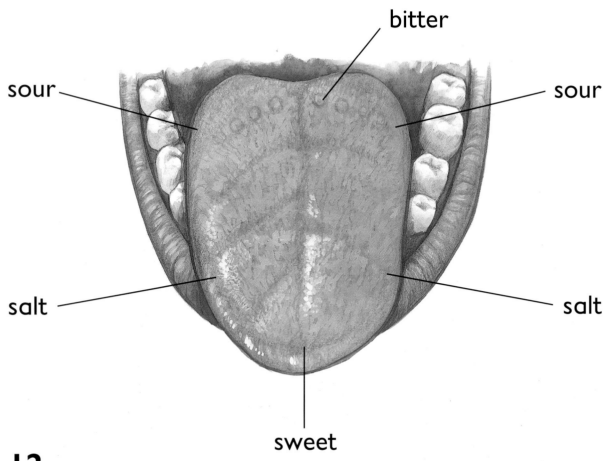

bitter

sour

sour

salt

salt

sweet

12

When you put something into your mouth, your tongue feels if it is hard or soft, hot or cold. Your tongue also feels if it is big and round.

WHY DO THINGS TASTE FUNNY?

Your brain needs smell and taste to get a **flavor**. Sometimes a bad head cold keeps you from being able to smell things. Then your food tastes funny.

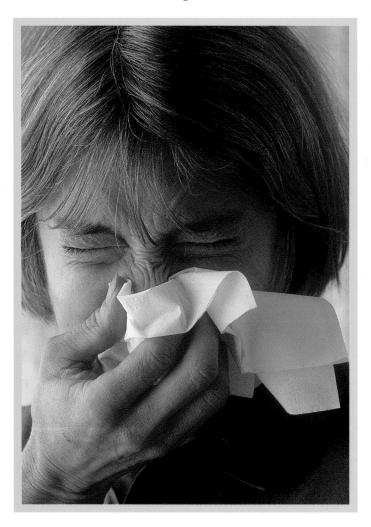

Hot things can burn the **taste buds**. Cold things, such as a popsicle, can **numb** the taste buds. When this happens, the taste buds cannot taste things for a while.

HOW ANIMALS USE TASTE

Some animals have **taste buds** that work like yours. Chimpanzees like some of the same food that you eat. They taste things the same way that you taste things.

Some animals like things that taste sweeter than sugar. Hummingbirds like to sip **nectar** from flowers. Insects, such as butterflies, like the taste of nectar, too.

MORE ABOUT ANIMALS

Many insects can taste sweet, sour, salt, and bitter, just like you. Many animals like the taste of plants. Giraffes like the taste of tender tree leaves.

A sheep's tongue can taste many different **flavors** in a clump of grass.

UNUSUAL WAYS TO TASTE

Most animals have **receptors** that taste their food. A spider has special **antennae** called **pedipalps** to taste things. Butterflies and honeybees taste with their feet.

Lizards and snakes have a receptor in the **roof** of the mouth to smell and taste things. A snake flicks its tongue and pushes air onto the receptor to taste it.

USING TASTE TO KEEP SAFE

Cats and dogs, like most animals, smell their food before they taste it. If it smells bad, they do not eat it. If they taste something they do not like, they spit it out.

Parrots have **taste buds**. They can taste their food. But most birds do not have taste buds. Ostriches eat anything that fits in their mouth and goes down their throat.

INVESTIGATING TASTE

Look carefully at someone's tongue. Do you see the little bumps? These are **taste buds**.

Look at the picture. Which of these things do you think will taste salty, sour, sweet, or bitter?

PLAYING TRICKS ON TASTE

Your taste messages travel to the brain more slowly than other messages. If you smell an onion while you eat an apple, your brain tells you that you are eating an onion!

If food looks different, you might think it tastes different, too. Eyes send a message to the brain more quickly than **taste buds** do. Would you like the taste of green potato?

DID YOU KNOW?

An adult has about three thousand **taste buds**. A child has even more! Taste buds die as you grow older. Older people are less **sensitive** to taste than children are.

When you think about eating something, your mouth makes **saliva**. This helps you taste things. In your lifetime, you will make enough saliva to fill a swimming pool!

GLOSSARY

antenna (more than one are called antennae) long, thin growths that help some animals know what is around them

chemical what a thing is made up of

flavor the way something tastes

nectar sweet, sugary juice inside flowers

nerve something that carries messages from the body to the brain

numb not able to feel

receptor cell in the body that can sense what is around it

roof the top of the inside of the mouth

pedipalp special part of a spider's body that looks like a leg but is used to taste food

saliva water made in the mouth that keeps the mouth wet and helps digest food

sensitive able to feel or sense quickly and strongly

taste bud group of cells on the outside of the tongue

SENSE MAP

5. The brain recognizes the taste.

1. The tongue feels the shape of the food.

2. Taste **receptors** (**taste buds**) are on the tongue.

3. Saliva comes from under the tongue to make food wet enough to swallow.

4. Nerves carry the message to the brain.

MORE BOOKS TO READ

Cromwell, Sharon. *How Do I Know It's Yucky? And Other Questions about the Senses.* Des Plaines, Ill.: Rigby Interactive Library, 1998.

Pluckrose, Henry. *Eating and Tasting.* Austin, Tex.: Raintree Steck-Vaughn, 1998.

Pringle, Laurence. *Taste.* Tarrytown, N.Y.: Marshall Cavendish, 1999.

INDEX